RISE TODAY

TRUSTING GOD AND HIS PROMISE

JASON F. WRIGHT

ENSIGN
PEAK

For Ron Zirkle

Because his example and personal ministry

have taught me to rise again, and again,

and again.

HE.
IS.
RISEN.

Those three words are more than a headline.

They are a promise.

Because He is risen, we too shall rise again.

But what if the message of the RESURRECTION is about more than the reuniting of body and soul?

What if the process of rising again can begin TODAY?

Every child of God has moments when it seems as if a GIANT ROCK has been rolled in front of our path.

You may have heard these whisperings . . .

"I CANNOT OVERCOME."

"I AM DONE TRYING."

"I CANNOT RISE AGAIN."

You may feel emotionally whipped
by winds beyond your control.

You might be reading this right now
and thinking that your own saving miracle is
TOO FAR AWAY to lean on.

If you feel ALONE, in the dark,
and powerless, remember this . . .

Rising again doesn't need to wait
until body and soul reunite.

HE IS RISEN

so we can rise...

TODAY.

Christ is willing to move the rock right now. He is desperate to HELP US RISE.

He longs for us to pray, to surrender our sorrows, our guilt, our habits, and our heartache.

HE IS THE HOPE!

All He requires is our heart and will.

No matter how much faith you have, it is enough.

Because Jesus Christ loves you.

PERFECTLY.

Listen to these divine whisperings . . .

"I am loved."

"I can do all things in Christ."

"I will rise because of Him."

"HE. IS. RISEN."

If you choose today to rise,
CHRIST WILL NOT
LEAVE YOUR SIDE
as you step out from your tomb
and into the light.

If you choose today to rise, you
have friends and loved ones
here for you—some you can see,
and some you cannot.

If you choose today to allow Christ more fully into your life, to accept His grace, to believe in His name . . .

You will begin to rise. Little by little. Your light will grow brighter.

ALL BECAUSE HE IS RISEN.

Rejoice! A marvelous Resurrection is
coming for all of us.

But you need not wait for that miracle
to rise in every other way.

RISE TODAY.

Prayer.

Throughout my life I've been blessed with wonderful friends and family who love to listen. When I failed the seventh grade, my father listened to my fears. When he died a few years later, my mother and siblings listened patiently as I navigated my grief. Today my wife, children, and close friends are willing to listen when I need to rise again from failure. You likely have similar people in your life.

There's another I've learned to rely on. In fact, He reigns at the center of my support system. I've found that no friend, no family member, and no professional is as willing to listen and provide comfort as my Father in Heaven. Praying with real intent, taking our time, and letting a spiritual discussion develop provide strength we can never measure. Like those others who love us, He is ready to hear you. And he's never too busy to hear your voice.

Reading God's word.

I love personal letters. There's something about seeing a friend's heart and soul spelled out on paper that moves me. I receive thousands of letters each year and I save and savor every single one. I always do my best to respond, because I think it demonstrates how much the sender means to me.

A few years ago, I finally began to think of the scriptures the same way. I'd always known that much of the New Testament was a collection of letters. Twenty-one of the twenty-seven books are letters—epistles—mostly from Paul. But when I began to think of all the scriptures as letters from a loving God to His children, it changed the way I saw them. If you want to know God's plan for you, if you're ready to accept His path for healing and second chances, if you want to demonstrate how much He means to you, read God's letters written by His apostles and prophets. They are timeless and miraculously personalized. Just for you.

Listening to sacred music.

For years I've had a playlist called Sunday Tunes. Believe it or not, some of the songs I've played more than 400 times. While editing a particularly spiritual column during the height of the pandemic, I swapped out one of my typical playlists for that trusted friend: Sunday Tunes. The Spirit and inspiration came in a rush, and my writing sessions have never been the same. As I write these very words at the back of this book, I'm listening to one of about a dozen playlists ranging from traditional hymns to popular Christian music.

Instead of listening to and singing hymns and other sacred music only on the Sabbath, consider making this joyful noise a part of your daily routine. Feeling down in your daily commute? Stream hymns on your phone. Working around the house as you ponder your life's trials? Play your favorite Christian band or choir loud enough to hear in every room. Make music that invites the Spirit the soundtrack of your life. Remember that when you lift Him in song, you're lifting yourself too.

Worshiping with others.

If you'd visited the congregation I attended fifteen years ago, you would have found me in the back row of every meeting, often with a pew or two between me and anyone else. It wasn't that I didn't like people, it's that I came to church and disappeared into my own spiritual questions and quiet musings. One Sunday afternoon at church, a man I admired deeply stood at the pulpit and invited all of us in the back row to stand up and come to the front and to sit side by side, with no space between us. Most of us did, and I've never been the same. The visual lesson of gathering with my spiritual siblings turned into a spiritual lesson.

We might consider that, as Christ invited others to engage, gather, and follow Him, His body of believers grew. Hearts were changed. Miracles unfolded. Healing and strength come when we worship with those who have similar fears, dreams, mistakes to overcome, and victories to celebrate. And may we never forget why church attendance matters so much. It's unclear who said it first, but the quote is timeless: "A church is a hospital for sinners, not a museum for saints."

Service.

When I was young, I had a gift for serving on the edges. I was dragged to every service project, helped move countless families in or out, and reluctantly stayed after every church potluck to put away chairs. But I realized over time that I was barely dipping a toe in the pool of sacrifice. My arms and hands were in the room, but my heart wasn't.

Thankfully, friends and mentors modeled real service for me through the years and taught me that to learn to love others, and to draw closer to God, I needed to immerse my heart in the service of others. I had to lose myself and find others by giving up time, talents, and sometimes treasure. It took work, but I discovered that the more I looked beyond myself and cared for other people's needs, the more I felt God caring for mine.

OTHER BOOKS BY
JASON F. WRIGHT

The James Miracle

Christmas Jars

Christmas Jars Reunion

Christmas Jars Journey

Penny's Christmas Jar Miracle

Recovering Charles

The Cross Gardener

The Seventeen Second Miracle

The 13th Day of Christmas

The Wednesday Letters

The Wedding Letters

Picturing Christmas

The Christmas Jukebox

Even the Dog Knows

Until You Find Strength

IMAGE CREDITS

Visit us at shadowmountain.com

ENSIGN PEAK is an imprint of Shadow Mountain Publishing, LLC.

ISBN 978-1-63993-110-1

Printed in China
RR Donnelley, Dongguan, China

10 9 8 7 6 5 4 3 2 1